DO YOU PRAY?

A question for everybody

J C RYLE

LIGHTLY EDITED & UPDATED BY MARY DAVIS

EP Books (Evangelical Press), Registered Office: 140
Coniscliffe Road, Darlington, Co Durham DL3 7RT
admin@epbooks.org
www.epbooks.org

EP Books are distributed in the USA by:
JPL Books, 3883 Linden Ave. S.E., Wyoming, MI 49548
orders@jplbooks.com
www.jplbooks.com

© EP Books 2018.
This revision first published 2018

British Library Cataloguing in Publication Data available
ISBN 978-1-78397-217-3

DO YOU PRAY?

A question for everybody

DO YOU PRAY?

CONTENTS

DO YOU PRAY?
A QUESTION FOR EVERYBODY

And he told them a parable to the effect that they ought always to pray and not lose heart. (Luke 18:1)

I desire then that in every place the men should pray (1 Timothy 2:8)

I want to ask you an exceptionally important question. It is the title of this short book and it is contained in just three words: Do you pray?

Only you can answer that question. Your minister knows whether you attend public worship or not. Your relatives know whether you have family prayers at home or not. Your friends may know whether you pray with other people. But only you know whether you pray in private. That is a matter between just you and God.

I beg you to think carefully about this. Please do not say that the question is too personal. If your heart is right in God's sight, it should not be a problem. There is nothing to be worried about. Please do not try to sidestep my question by saying that you 'say your prayers'. We all know that it is one thing to say your prayers, and another thing entirely to 'pray'. And please do not tell me that my question is unnecessary. Bear with me a little while longer, and I will show you that I have some very good reasons for asking it.

I. I ASK, 'DO YOU PRAY?' BECAUSE PRAYER IS ABSOLUTELY NECESSARY TO A PERSON'S SALVATION

I say, 'absolutely necessary'—and I am choosing my words carefully. (Let me say that I am not speaking about children, nor those who have limited understanding, nor of the unbeliever who has never heard the gospel. I am fully aware that where little is given, little will be required.) I am talking about those who call themselves Christians. And I sincerely believe that if a person does not pray, they cannot expect to be saved.

Let me say that I believe in salvation by grace as strongly as anyone. I would gladly offer a free and full pardon to the greatest sinner that ever lived. I would not hesitate to stand by their deathbed, and say, 'Believe in the Lord Jesus Christ, even now, and you will be saved.' I am a firm believer in salvation by grace. But I cannot see anything at all in the Bible that says someone could have salvation without asking for it. If someone will not even lift up their hearts to the Lord and say, 'Lord Jesus, give it to me', I cannot see how that person can possibly expect to be saved.

The Bible never says that somebody will be saved *by* their prayers – I am sure of that. But at the same time, I cannot see anything in the Bible that says somebody will be saved *without* prayer.

It is not *absolutely necessary* to salvation that a person should read the Bible. A person may be totally illiterate, but still have Christ in their heart. It is not *absolutely necessary* that someone should listen to sermons or hear the public preaching of the gospel. They may live where the gospel is not preached, they may be totally bedridden and unable to get to church, they may be completely deaf and be unable to hear. However, the same thing cannot be said about prayer. It is *absolutely necessary* to salvation that a person should pray.

Prayer is something we each need to do for ourselves. It is the same with our health and our learning. You cannot get someone else to eat, drink or sleep for you. You cannot get someone else to learn the alphabet for you. They are all things that we need to do *for ourselves.* Otherwise they will not be done at all. It is the same with the soul. There are certain things which are absolutely necessary to the soul's health and well-being. And everyone must see to these things *for*themselves. Each man must repent for himself. Each woman must approach Christ for herself. Each must speak to God and pray for himself or herself. *You* must do it for yourself; nobody else can do it for you. How can you expect to be saved by an unknown God? And how can you know God without prayer? When it comes to human friendships, you cannot know a person unless you talk to them. Similarly, you cannot know God in Christ unless you speak to him in prayer. If you want to be with him in heaven, you must be one of his friends on earth. If you want to be one of his friends on earth, you must pray.

There will be a huge crowd at Christ's right hand on the last day. Believers will come from the north and south, from the east and west, and there will be a multitude that no-one can count. The song of victory that will burst from their mouths will be a glorious song! It will be far greater than the noise of the oceans, far greater than the noise of the mightiest thunderstorm. But there will not be a note out of place in that song. Those who sing will sing with one heart and one voice. Their experience will be one and the same. All of them will have believed. All of them will have been washed clean by the blood of Jesus Christ. All of them will have been born again. All of them will have prayed.

We must pray on earth, or we shall never praise in heaven. Or let me put it this way, we must go through the school of prayer or we shall never be fit for the holiday of praise. Let me tell you, the prayerless person will be without God, without Christ, without grace, without hope and without heaven. It is to be on the road to hell. Strong words certainly. But then there are such serious consequences. So, I hope you are not surprised that I ask you: Do you pray?

2. I ASK, 'DO YOU PRAY?' BECAUSE A HABIT OF PRAYER IS ONE OF THE SUREST MARKS OF A TRUE CHRISTIAN

Each child of God is alike in this respect: from the moment there is any life and reality to their faith, they pray. Just as the very first sign of life in a new baby is the act of breathing, so the first act of men and women when they are born again is praying. One of the most common marks of all who trust in God is to pray—or, as the Bible puts it, to 'cry to him day and night'.[1] The Holy Spirit makes us new creatures and adopts us into God's family, and he leads us cry out to him, 'Abba, Father'.[2] When the Lord Jesus gives us life, he gives us a voice and a tongue, and says to us, 'Do not be silent anymore.' God does not have any silent children. That is because, when someone becomes a child of God, it is part of their new nature to pray, just as it is part of a new-born

1   Luke 18:7
2   Romans 8:15

baby's nature to cry. God's children see their need of mercy and grace. They feel their emptiness and weakness. They cannot do anything else to help themselves. They must pray.

I have looked carefully at the lives of believers in the Bible. I cannot find a single one (where we know something of their lives) who was not a person of prayer. Quite the opposite. It is often said of the godly that they 'call on him as Father' or 'call upon the name of our Lord Jesus Christ'; we are told that the wicked, on the other hand, 'do not call upon the Lord'. [3]

I have read about the lives of many well-known Christians who have lived since the Bible days. Some were rich, others were poor. Some were clever, others were not. Some of them were from one branch of the church, others from a different one. Some loved formal church services and liturgy, others preferred spontaneity and informality. But I see one thing that they all had in common. They were all men and women of prayer. I have read many reports from missionary societies. It is wonderful to see how unbelievers from all over the world are receiving the gospel. There are conversions in Africa, in Asia, in the Americas. Those who become Christians are often very different from one another. But I notice one striking thing that they have in common: converted people always pray.

I am fully aware that people can pray without engaging their heart. I know that people can pray without sincerity. And I do not pretend that just because a person prays, it proves anything at all about their soul. As with every other aspect of faith and religion,

---

3   1 Peter 1:17, 1 Corinthians 1:2, Psalm 14:4

there is plenty of room for deception and hypocrisy here too. But I do say this: *not* praying is a clear proof that someone is not yet a true Christian. He or she cannot really feel his or her sins. They cannot love God. They cannot feel themselves to be in debt to Christ. They cannot long after holiness. They cannot desire heaven. They cannot yet have been born again. They cannot yet have been made a new creature. They may boast confidently of having faith, grace, election, hope and knowledge—and they may well deceive some people. But, if that person does not pray, you can be sure that it is all empty talk.

What is more, when it comes to the indwelling of the Holy Spirit, one of the best pieces of evidence of his work is a habit of heartfelt private prayer. A Christian may preach, they may write best-selling books, make brilliant speeches and do endless good works and yet still be like Judas Iscariot who betrayed Jesus. But, a believer who goes into their room and pours out their soul before God in secret will not often do that that unless they are in earnest.

The Lord Jesus himself pointed to prayer as proof of Saul's conversion. In Acts 9, God gave Ananias only one piece of evidence of Saul's change of heart: 'he is praying'.[4] I know that a lot of things may go on in someone's mind before they start to pray. They may have many strong feelings, intentions, resolutions, convictions, desires, wishes, hopes and fears. But none of these things is necessarily evidence of a true change of heart. You can find all those things in unbelievers, and they often come to nothing. Often, they last no longer than the morning mist, or the dew that disap-

4   Acts 9:11

pears with the rising sun. A heartfelt prayer which flows from a broken and contrite spirit is worth all these things put together.

The Bible teaches us that God's elect are chosen for salvation from before all eternity. It tells us that the Holy Spirit often leads them to relationship with Christ step by step. We do not know the mind of God and we can only judge by what we see. For my own mind, I cannot be confident that anyone is justified until they repent and believe. And I could never be sure that someone truly believes until he or she prays. I cannot see how a silent, speechless, uncommunicative faith can be real faith.

The first act of faith will be to speak to God. A person cannot possibly live without breathing; nor can they possibly believe without praying. With that in mind, please do not be surprised if you hear your church leaders talking a lot about the importance of prayer. The reason is, we want to be sure that you pray. You may have incredibly sound doctrine and you may love the Bible—but it is quite possible for this to be nothing more than head-knowledge. Your love for the church and other Christians may be especially warm—but that could just be love for a particular sub-culture. The vital question is whether you are actually acquainted with the throne of grace, whether you can speak *to* God as well as speak *about* him. Do you want to know whether you are a true Christian? Then please realise that this question is exceptionally important: Do you pray?

3. I ASK, 'DO YOU PRAY?' BECAUSE PRIVATE PRAYER IS THE MOST NEGLECTED CHRISTIAN DISCIPLINE

Many people in the world today call themselves Christians. They go to public worship and attend many different types of churches. Some branches of the church are really growing. But, despite all this, I think there is a huge neglect of private prayer. I would not always have said that. I once thought that most people 'said their prayers' and that many people 'prayed'. Now I have changed my views and concluded that most professing Christians do not pray at all. This may sound rather shocking and somewhat surprising to you.

The problem is that prayer is one of those things which we think will happen automatically—so, of course, it is shamefully neglected. We feel that prayer is a 'shared responsibility' in our churches and, as often happens when we have shared responsibility, we leave it to others and very few of us take on the responsibility to pray. Private prayer is a personal business between God and our souls—something which no-one else sees. It is not a surprise, then, that there is a huge temptation to bypass prayer completely.

I think there are thousands who never say a word of prayer at all, even among those who call themselves Christians. We eat. We drink. We sleep. We get up in the morning. We go to work. We go home. We take exercise. We breathe God's air. We enjoy God's sun. We walk on God's earth. We experience God's mercies. We have bodies that are dying. And we have judgment and eternity before us. But some of us never speak to God. We behave like animals—animals that just live and then die. We live like creatures without souls. We do not have a word for the God whose hand holds our life, breath and everything else. Not a word for the one who will pronounce our everlasting sentence one day. That is dreadful, isn't it? If all our secrets were out in the open, I think we would find that it is very common.

I think there are tens of thousands of people whose prayers are nothing but a formality, an empty shell, a few words spoken with no thought as to their meaning. Some might mumble some sentences remembered from their childhood. Others may say the Lord's Prayer, without really expecting answers to the solemn requests in it. Some people may mutter a quick prayer after they have collapsed into bed at night, or scramble over their prayers while getting ready in the morning. We may sure that, in God's sight, this is not praying.

Words said without engaging the heart are as utterly useless to our souls as the incessant beating of a drum, as useless as sending a love-letter written by a stranger to *your* loved-one. Words may be said, lips may be moving, but where there is no heart, there is nothing that God listens to—there is no prayer. I have no doubt that Saul said many a long prayer before the Lord met him on the way to Damascus. But, remember that it was not till his heart was broken that the Lord said, 'he is praying'.

Does this surprise you? I realise the seriousness of what I am saying and, believe me, I am convinced by it. Perhaps you find it rather excessive—maybe, in your opinion, it is totally wrong. Please consider carefully what I am saying, and I hope I will soon be able to convince you that I am simply telling you the truth.

I wonder if you have forgotten that it is not a *natural* thing for someone to pray. The human mind is hostile to God. When it comes to our hearts, we naturally want to get as far away from God as possible and have nothing to do with him. Our feelings toward God are not naturally those of love. And why should someone pray if they have no sense of sin, no sense of spiritual need, no conviction of unseen things, no genuine desire for holiness and no longing for heaven? Naturally speaking, most people know nothing and feel nothing when it comes to all these things. People naturally follow the crowd, and the crowd always takes the easiest route. That is the way it is, and it is one reason that I believe that few people really pray.

Prayer is not a *fashionable* thing either. Most of us would not rush to talk to others about our prayer lives. We would rather talk about our successes or our latest passion than tell the rest of the office or the classroom that we pray. If you ended up sharing a room on holiday with someone you did not know very well, would you be too embarrassed to pray before you went to sleep? Thousands of Christians would. Being popular and successful, looking good, being at the right parties, being thought clever and acceptable—these things are considered fashionable; praying certainly is not. That is just the way it is. If people are reluctant to admit to personal prayer when they are in public, I cannot believe that it is a very popular practice in private. That is another reason I believe that few people really pray.

And what about our lifestyles? Can we believe that people are praying against sin both night and day when we see them plunging right into it? Can we suppose they pray against worldly thinking, when they are entirely absorbed and taken up with it? Can we think they are really asking God for grace to serve him, when they show no desire at all to do so? No, we cannot. It is as plain as day that most people either ask nothing of God or, if they do pray, they cannot possibly mean what they say. Praying and sinning will never live together in the same heart. Either prayer will consume sin, or sin will choke prayer. That is just how it is. I look at people's lives and I come to the conclusion that few people really pray.

What about the way that those who are nearing death often seem to be complete strangers to God? They are sadly ignorant of the gospel. They are sadly unused to speaking to God, even unable to. There is often a dreadful awkwardness, a shyness and a rawness in their attempts to approach the Lord. It is as if they are trying to take up a completely new habit or hobby. They seem to need someone to introduce them to God, as if they are meeting someone completely new, someone they have never talked to before.

I remember hearing about a lady who wanted a minister to visit her before she died. She wanted him to pray with her, so he asked her what he should pray for. She did not know. She could not think of anything she wanted him to pray for. She just knew she wanted a minister to pray – that is all. I quite understand this. Death-beds have a way of revealing secrets. That is how it often is with those who are facing death. And it is another reason that I conclude that few people pray.

I cannot see into your heart—of course I can't. I do not know your personal story when it comes to spiritual things. But from what I see in the Bible and in the world, I am sure this is the most important question I can put to you: Do you pray?

4. I ASK, 'DO YOU PRAY?' BECAUSE THE BIBLE IS FULL OF ENCOURAGEMENT FOR ALL WHO WANT TO PRAY

God does everything he possibly can to make prayer easy, if we will only try it. Everything is sorted on his side. Every objection is dealt with. Every difficulty is provided for. The prophet Isaiah tells us that the 'uneven ground' will become level and the 'rough places' made into a plain.[5] Or we might say that the roads are beautifully straight and smooth, and all the pot-holes are filled in. That means that there is no excuse for any of us who does not pray. A way has been made for each of us, however sinful and unworthy we are, to draw near to God the Father. Jesus Christ has opened that way by his atoning sacrifice for us on the cross. So, we do not need to be frightened by God's holiness and justice; they are no reason for us to keep away from him. We only need to cry to God in Jesus' name and we will find him upon a throne of grace, ready and willing to hear us. The name of Jesus is like a passport that always guarantees entry for our prayers. In Jesus' name, each of us is able to draw near to God with boldness and approach him with confidence. He has promised to hear us. That is wonderfully encouraging.

We have an advocate, someone who will represent us and act for us. We have an intercessor who will speak on our behalf. It is Jesus Christ himself, and he is waiting to present our prayers, if only we will ask him to. He mingles our feeble prayers with his own almighty prayers and, together, they go as a sweet aroma to the throne of God. By themselves, our prayers are poor and weak. But in Jesus' hand, they are mighty and powerful. He is our high priest and our elder brother. Think of a legal contract, a bank note or a cheque: without the proper signature, it is nothing but a worthless piece of paper. The signature gives it value. Similarly, the prayers of a believer are worthless, feeble and weak, but once they are in the hand of our Lord Jesus, they have value and can achieve great things. Apparently, there used to be army officers serving in Rome who had an 'open-door policy' so that they could always be available to any Roman citizen who asked for help. In the same sort of way, Jesus' door is always open to every single person who calls on him for mercy and grace. Helping believers is his particular role, and their prayers are his delight. That is wonderfully encouraging.

We are weaklings when it comes to prayer, but the Holy Spirit is always ready to help us. He is by our side as we try to speak with God. We do not need to be worried about knowing what to say. The Spirit will give us the words and inspire our prayers. Those who belong to the Lord have good reasons to believe that they will be heard. It is not just that we are praying, but the fact that the Holy Spirit is pleading on our behalf. That is wonderfully encouraging.

In the Bible, there are very precious and encouraging promises to all those who pray. Think carefully about what Jesus meant when he said these things:

> *Ask, and it will be given to you; seek, and you will find; knock, and it will be opened to you. For everyone who asks receives, and the one who seeks finds, and to the one who knocks it will be opened.*[6]

> *And whatever you ask in prayer, you will receive, if you have faith.*[7]

> *Whatever you ask in my name, this I will do, that the Father may be glorified in the Son. If you ask me anything in my name, I will do it.*[8]

And what about the parable of the man who visits his friend at midnight and will not go away until he gets the help he wants?[9] Or the parable of the persistent widow who would not give up until the judge gave her justice?[10] What is the Lord's message to us

---

6   Matthew 7:7-8
7   Matthew 21:22
8   John 14:13-14
9   Luke 11:5
10   Luke 18:1

in those passages? If we cannot see any encouragement to pray in all these verses, then words have no meaning at all!

There are also great *examples* in the Bible of the power of prayer. It seems that nothing is too great or too difficult when it comes to prayer. Prayer achieves things that would otherwise be completely impossible and out of reach. In the Bible, we read that prayer opened the Red Sea.[11] Prayer brought water from a rock[12] and bread from heaven[13]. Prayer made the sun stand still.[14] Prayer brought fire from the sky onto Elijah's sacrifice at Carmel.[15] Prayer overthrew armies.[16] Prayer has healed the sick.[17] Prayer has raised the dead.[18] In church history, we read about Mary Queen of Scots who apparently said, 'I fear John Knox's prayers more than an army of ten thousand men.' Prayer has brought about the conversion of souls. 'The child of many prayers,' said an old Christian to Augustine's mother, 'shall never perish.' Prayer and faith can do anything. Nothing is impossible when a person has the spirit of adoption. While Abraham continued to ask for mercy for Sodom, the Lord went on giving. He never stopped giving until Abraham stopped praying.[19] That is wonderfully encouraging.

What else could we possibly need to encourage us to pray? What more could God do to pave the way to his mercy-seat?

---

11   Exodus 14:16-17, 21-22
12   Numbers 20:1-13
13   Exodus 16
14   Joshua 10:1-15
15   1 Kings 18:36
16   2 Kings 19:20-36
17   Matthew 8:5-17
18   John 11:38-44
19   Genesis 18:16-33

What more could he do to remove the chance of us stumbling along the way? How can we neglect such great encouragement? If we die without prayer after all this, I am not sure we can have any excuse. I do not want any of us to be prayerless. And I am sure you understand why I put this question to you: Do you pray?

5. I ASK, 'DO YOU PRAY?' BECAUSE FAITHFULNESS IN PRAYER IS THE SECRET OF TRUE HOLINESS

There is, undoubtedly, a big difference among true Christians. To use a military analogy, there is a huge difference between those leading the charge in God's army and those who bring up the rear. They are all fighting the same good fight—but some are fighting much more boldly than others. They are all doing the Lord's work—but some are much more hard-working. They are all 'light in the Lord'—but some shine so much more brightly. They run the same race—but some get on so much faster than others. They all love the same Lord and Saviour—but some love him so much more.

It is true, isn't it? Some people become Christians but they never seem to make much progress from that moment on. They are born again, but they remain spiritual babies all their lives.

They are learners in Christ's school, but they never seem to get beyond their 'ABC' and they never progress beyond the first year of school. Year after year, you notice the same old sins—they never move on. They have no new experiences of the Lord which they can speak about. They never develop a hearty spiritual appetite. They are lazy when it comes to forming Biblical views on tricky issues. Like babies, they will not have anything but the 'milk' of the word and they will only listen to simple teaching which fits in with their views.[20] They dislike 'solid food' and they will not think through anything difficult or challenging. They want to be like Peter Pan, never growing up, never getting wiser or stronger. They are only interested in what affects them and their own little circle. I say this with great sadness. But I ask any real Christian, is it not true?

You come across other Christians who are the absolute opposite. They always seem to be growing and making progress. Growing like grass after summer rain. They go from strength to strength, their faith deepens, their character becomes more and more Christ-like. Every time you meet them, their hearts seem larger and they have grown in spiritual stature. Every year, they seem to see more, know more, believe more and feel more when it comes to their faith. They have good works to prove the reality of their faith, and they are zealous to do more. They attempt great things, and achieve great things. When they fail, they try again, and when they fall, they want to pick themselves up again. But, if you were to ask them, you would find that they do not think highly of themselves, they are deeply aware of their sin, and

20   Hebrews 5:12

they think that they contribute very little. These Christians make Christianity attractive and beautiful in other people's eyes. Even unbelievers notice! Sometimes, even the most selfish person will admit their goodness. They are the kind of people who it is always good to see, to be with and to listen to. You feel better from just being with them. When you meet them, you might conclude that they had just been in God's presence (like Moses in the book of Exodus).[21] When you say your goodbyes, you feel encouraged by their company, as if your soul had been near a warm campfire. I know such people are rare, but I am sure you know the kind of people I mean.

What accounts for differences like these? Why are some believers so much brighter and holier than others? Nineteen times out of twenty, I believe the difference comes from different habits in private prayer. I think that those who are not truly holy, pray very little; and those who are truly holy, pray a lot. My views may surprise you. I know that many people think that true holiness is a kind of special gift, which only a few people achieve. They admire it at a distance; they may aspire to it when they read about it in books; they think it is beautiful when they see an example nearer home. But they assume it is exceptionally rare. They think it must be a kind of exclusive gift which is given to just a few special believers, but certainly not to everybody.

I think this view is dangerously wrong. I believe that spiritual greatness (and natural greatness too, in fact) depends mostly on how we use the gifts and resources that God gives us. I am not

---

21   Exodus 34:35

saying, of course, that we can all expect a miraculous gift of intelligence when we turn to Christ. But I do believe that the Lord gives us the means to become holy when we put our trust in him. Then it is mostly a matter of whether we will be faithful, careful and earnest in pursuing holiness.

And I am sure that the most important means by which most believers have become great in the Christ's church is the habit of faithful, private prayer. Look at the lives of the brightest and best of God's servants, whether in the Bible or not. See what is said of Moses, of David, of Daniel and of Paul. Notice what is written about Martin Luther and John Bradford, two of the great Reformers. Look at what we know about the private devotions of people like George Whitefield and Murray M'Cheyne. You will be able to think of many others. But I challenge you to tell me of one great man or woman of God who was not a man or woman of prayer!

Depend on it, prayer is power! Prayer brings a fresh and continued out-pouring of the Spirit. It is the Holy Spirit alone who begins the work of grace in someone's heart. He alone can carry that work forward and make it prosper. But the good Spirit loves to be asked and entreated. And those who ask most will always have most of his influence.[22]

Prayer is the most effective remedy against the Devil and against persistent sins. The Devil will not be able to keep dominion over us when we beg the Lord to banish him. Those sins will never stand up to heartfelt prayer. But we must spread out

---

22   Luke 11:11-13

everything before God our heavenly doctor if he is to give us daily comfort and relief. We must drag our indwelling sins to the feet of Christ, and beg him to send them where they belong. Do you genuinely want to grow in grace and be a truly holy Christian? If you do, there is no more important question than this: Do you pray?

6. I ASK, 'DO YOU PRAY?' BECAUSE NEGLECTING PRAYER IS ONE OF THE GREAT CAUSES OF BACKSLIDING

t is quite possible to backslide in the Christian faith after making a good start. Believers may run well for a time, like the Galatians did, and then turn aside to follow false teachers.[23] They may talk about their faith enthusiastically while their feelings are warm and vibrant, just like Peter did; and then, when trials and difficulties come, they may deny their Lord.[24] Believers may lose their first love, as the Ephesians did.[25] They may cool down in their zeal to do good, like Mark, Paul's companion.[26] They may follow the apostle's teaching for a while, and then, go back to the world like Demas did.[27] Believers may do all these things.

---

23   Galatians 1:6
24   Matthew 26:35, 69-75
25   Revelation 2:4
26   Acts 15:38
27   2 Timothy 4:10

It is a really miserable thing to be a backslider. In fact, I think it is one of the very worst and most unhappy things that can happen to a believer. It is a sad sight—like a stranded ship, a broken-winged eagle, a garden over-run with weeds, a harp without strings, a church in ruins. These are all sad sights, but a backslider is an even sadder sight. I have no doubt that true grace will never be extinguished, and true union with Christ will never be broken off. But I do believe that someone can fall so far away from Christ that they lose sight of their own grace, and despair of their own salvation. And if this is not hell, it is certainly the next thing to it. A wounded conscience, a mind which is sick of itself, a memory which is full of self-reproach, a heart pierced through with the Lord's arrows, a spirit broken with a load of inward accusation— all these are a taste of hell. It is a hell on earth. The solemn saying of the wise man in Proverbs is important, 'The backslider in heart will be filled with the fruit of his ways.'[28]

Now what is the cause of most backsliding? I think that one of the main reasons is a neglect of private prayer. Of course, the secrets of exactly why believers stumble and fall will not be known until the last day. I simply give my opinion as a minister of Christ and as someone who studies the way of faith. I believe that backsliding generally starts with a failure to pray. Reading our Bibles without prayer, listening to sermons without prayer, carrying on marriages without prayer, choosing houses without prayer, travelling without prayer, forming friendships without prayer, hurrying over our daily prayers, saying them without engaging our hearts. There are many other examples we could think of. They are all

---

28   Proverbs 14:14

downward steps by which it is very easy to descend into spiritual apathy, downward steps to a place where God allows us to have a tremendous fall. In the Bible, we see this again and again. You can read about the lingering Lots, the unstable Samsons, the wife-idolising Solomons, the inconsistent Asas, the pliable Jehoshaphats, the over-careful Marthas.[29] And there are so many like them to be found in the Church of Christ. Often there is a very simple explanation—they became careless about private prayer.

You can be very sure that people fall in private, long before they fall in public. They are backsliders when it comes to their knees long before they backslide openly in the eyes of the world. Like Peter, they first ignore the Lord's warning to watch and pray; then, like Peter, their strength is gone and, when tempted, they deny their Lord. The world sees their fall and scoffs loudly. But the world knows nothing of the real reason.

If you do not want to be a backslider, think some more about my question: Do you pray?

---

29   Genesis 19:16, Judges 16:20, 1 Kings 11:1-16, 2 Chronicles 16:9, 2 Chronicles 20:35-37, Luke 10.

7. I ASK, 'DO YOU PRAY?' BECAUSE PRAYER IS THE BEST RECIPE FOR HAPPINESS AND CONTENTMENT

We live in a world full of sorrows. This has been the case ever since sin entered the Garden of Eden. Where there is sin, there is sorrow. And none of us can expect to escape sorrow until sin is driven out of the world. Some people have greater sorrows than others; that is certainly true. Few people manage to live long without sorrows or difficulties of one sort or another. Our bodies, our homes, our families, our children, our relatives, our friends, our colleagues, our neighbours, our work: each of these things are sources of both joys and sorrows. Sickness, death, loss, disappointment, separations, ingratitude, slander: these are all common. We cannot get through life without experiencing at least some of them. And the deeper our affections, the deeper our afflictions; and the more we love, the more we weep.

And what is the best recipe for cheerfulness in a world like this? How will we get through this valley of tears with least pain? I know no better solution than the habit of taking everything to God in prayer. This is what the Bible advises, in both the Old and New Testament.

> *The Psalmist reminds us, 'call upon me in the day of trouble; I will deliver you',*[30] *'Cast your burden on the Lord, and he will sustain you; he will never permit the righteous to be moved.'*[31]

> *The apostle Paul says, 'do not be anxious about anything, but in everything by prayer and supplication with thanksgiving let your requests be made known to God. And the peace of God, which surpasses all understanding, will guard your hearts and your minds in Christ Jesus.'*[32]

> *And the apostle James says, 'Is anyone among you suffering? Let him pray.'*[33]

That is what Jacob did when he feared his brother Esau.[34] It is what Moses did when the people were ready to stone him in the wilderness.[35] This is what Joshua did when Israel was defeated before Ai.[36] This is what David did when he was in danger at Keilah.[37] This is what Hezekiah did when he received the letter from

---

30   Psalm 50:15
31   Psalm 55:22
32   Philippians 4:6-7
33   James 5:13
34   Gen 32:11
35   Exodus 17:4
36   Joshua 7:7-9
37   1 Samuel 23:1-6

Sennacherib.[38] This is what the Church did when Peter was put in prison.[39] This is what Paul and Silas did when they were thrown into a cell at Philippi.[40]

The only way to be truly happy is to keep casting all our anxieties on God. If we try to carry our own burdens, it just makes us sad. If only we would tell God about our troubles and difficulties, he would help us bear them. If we are determined to carry them ourselves, one day we will find that even the lightest trouble feels like a huge burden.

We have a friend who is longing to help us if we will talk to him about our troubles. He is the perfect friend. A friend who showed his concern for the poor, the sick and the heavy-hearted when he lived on earth. A friend who knows our hearts because he lived as one of us for thirty-three years. A friend who can weep with those who weep because he was a 'man of sorrows', 'a man of suffering' and was 'acquainted with grief.'[41] A friend who can help us, because there is no pain he cannot cure, no difficulty he cannot deal with. That friend is Jesus Christ. And the way to be happy is to open our hearts to him, always, every day. Like the poor Christian who was unfairly threatened and brutally treated and simply said, 'I must tell the Lord.'

Jesus can satisfy those who trust him and call on him, he can make them truly happy, whatever their circumstances are. He can give peace of heart to the prisoner, contentment to the poor, com-

---

38   2 Kings 19:14-19
39   Acts 12:5
40   Acts 16:25
41   Isaiah 53:3

fort to those in the middle of the saddest bereavement, peace and joy even in the face of death. There is such fullness in Christ if we will put our trust in him, a fullness that will be poured out on everyone who will ask for it in prayer.

Happiness does not depend on our outward circumstances, but on the state of our hearts. Prayer can lighten our burdens; however heavy they are. It can call to our side the one who will help us to bear them. Prayer can open a door for us when the way ahead seems blocked. It can bring to our side our Lord who says, 'This is the way, walk in it.'[42] Prayer can let in a ray of hope when all our prospects seem dark. It can bring down that one who says, 'I will never leave you nor forsake you.'[43] Prayer can bring us relief when those we love are taken away and the world feels empty. It can bring down the one who can fill the gap in our hearts with himself, and say to the waves within us, 'Peace! Be still!'[44] We do not want to be like Hagar in the wilderness who could not see the well of living waters even though they were so close beside her.[45] Prayer is the secret of being a happy Christian and I know I cannot ask you a more useful question than this: Do you pray?

I hope and pray that you will think very carefully about what I have presented to you. I pray with all my heart that, as you do so, it will be a blessing to your soul. There is nothing more important.

---

42   Isaiah 30:21
43   Deuteronomy 31:8, Joshua 1:5
44   Mark 4:39
45   Genesis 21:19

A WORD TO THOSE
WHO DO NOT PRAY

L et me say something to those who do not pray. I do not assume that everyone who reads this will be a praying person. If you do not pray, let me say something particular to you on God's behalf. All I can do is to warn you and it is a very solemn warning. I want to warn you that you are in frightful danger. You must realise that if you die in your present state, you are a lost soul. The Bible warns us that those who die in their own sins face eternal misery—we will have no excuse if that is true of us.

Can you give me one good reason for living without prayer? It is useless to say you *do not know how to pray*. Praying is the very simplest act of faith. It is just speaking to God, no more than that. You do not need education or learning to start praying. You do not need wisdom, theology or a university degree. You need nothing but a willing and honest heart. The weakest child can cry when they are hungry—they do not worry about the words they use. The most ignorant person can find something to say to God, if they want to speak to him.

It is useless to say you *do not have a convenient place to pray*. Anyone can find a place private enough if they want to. Our Lord prayed on a mountain, Peter on a roof-top, Isaac in a field, Nathanael under a fig tree, Jonah in the stomach of a huge fish. Any place can be a place of prayer.

It is useless to say you *have no time*. There is plenty of time if we choose to make time. Time may be short but there is always enough time to pray. Daniel was in charge of all the affairs of the kingdom but he prayed three times a day. David was ruler over a mighty nation but he says, 'Evening and morning and at noon I utter my complaint and moan, and he hears my voice.'[46] When time is really needed, time can always be found.

It is useless to say you *cannot pray until you have faith and a new heart*, and that you must wait until then. This is to add sin to sin. It is a most terrible thing to be unconverted and to be facing eternal misery. It is even worse to say, 'I know that to be true, but I will not cry for mercy.' The Bible never condones that kind of thinking:

> *Isaiah said: 'Seek the Lord while he may be found; call upon him while he is near.'*[47]

---

46   Psalms 55:17
47   Isaiah 55:6

Hosea said: 'you have stumbled because of your iniquity.
Take with you words, and turn to the Lord: say unto him,
Take away all iniquity, and receive us graciously.'[48]

Peter said to Simon Magus: 'Repent, therefore, of this
wickedness of yours, and pray to the Lord.'[49]

If you want faith and a new heart, cry to the Lord for them. A simple prayer can bring life to a dead soul. If you know in your heart of hearts that you are a prayerless believer, why not pray to God now? Surely you do not want to make a deal with death and hell? Surely you have sins that need forgiving? Surely you are frightened of a dreadful eternity separated from God? Have you no desire at all for heaven? Please wake up and think about the end of your life! Please call on God!

I must warn you that there will be a day when many people will pray, 'Lord, Lord, open the door for us'—but it will be too late.[50] The Bible tells us that, on that day, the people who would not cry out to God during their lives will be crying to the rocks to fall on them and the hills to cover them.[51] I want to warn you because I do not want anyone to face that—I am not trying to frighten you or hurt you. Please make sure that this is not what awaits your soul. Salvation is very near you. Do not lose out on heaven because you never asked God.

---

48   Hosea 14:1-2
49   Acts 8:22
50   Matthew 25:11
51   Luke 23:30

A WORD TO THOSE WHO DO NOT KNOW WHERE TO START

N ow I want to say something to those who long for salvation but do know not what to do about it or where to begin. I think some readers may be in this situation. And, even if there is only one person like this, I want to offer you some warm encouragement and advice.

In every journey, there must be a first step. There must be a change from sitting down to standing up and moving forward. The Israelites' journey from Egypt to Canaan was long and tiring; forty years passed before they crossed the River Jordan. But there was a first step to that journey. One day, one of the Israelites took that first step on the journey out of Egypt. A person's first step in coming out from sin and the world is marked by their first heartfelt prayer. In every building, a first stone must be laid. The ark took 120 years to build, but there was a day when Noah raised his axe to fell the first tree. The temple of Solomon was a glorious building, but there was a day when the first huge stone was laid at the foot of Mount Moriah. When does the building of the Holy Spirit really begin to appear in someone's heart? It begins, so far as we can judge, when they first pour out their heart to God in prayer.

If you long for salvation and want to know what to do, let me give you this advice: go today (yes, today!) to the Lord Jesus Christ. Go to the first private place you can find, and beg him in prayer to save your soul. Tell him that you have heard that he receives sinners, and that he has said, 'whoever comes to me I will never cast out.'[52] Tell him that you are a poor, worthless sinner and that you come to him trusting in his invitation to you. Tell him you put yourself wholly and entirely in his hands. Tell him that you feel helpless and unworthy. Tell him that you feel hopeless in yourself. Tell him that unless he saves you, you have no possibility of being saved at all. Beg him to deliver you from the guilt, the power and the consequences of sin. Beg him to pardon you and wash you in his blood that was shed on the cross. Beg him to give you a new heart and plant the Holy Spirit in your soul. Beg him to give you the grace, the faith, the will and the power to be his disciple and servant from this day on.

If you are serious about your soul, go today (yes, today!) and speak to the Lord Jesus. Tell him in your own way, using your own words. If a doctor came to see you because you were feeling ill, I am sure you would be able to explain where you felt pain. If your soul feels its sin, I am sure you can find something to say to Jesus.

52   John 6:37

Do not think that he is unwilling to save you because you are a sinner. It is Christ's delight to save sinners. Remember his words, 'I have not come to call the righteous, but sinners to repentance'.[53] Do not put it off because you feel unworthy. Do not put it off for any reason at all. Do not put it off because of someone else. Encouragement to put off something this important comes only from the Devil.

Go to Christ, just as you are. The worse you are, the more you need to go to him! You will never be able to mend yourself by staying away. Do not be afraid because your prayers are not very fluent. Jesus can understand you. Mothers understand the first babblings of their babies, and our blessed Saviour Jesus understands sinners. He understands a sigh, and knows the meaning of a groan. Do not despair because you do not get an answer immediately. If you are speaking, Jesus is listening. If he delays an answer, it is for a good reason, perhaps to make sure you are in earnest. Pray on and the answer will come. Although it may take a while, keep waiting for it. His answer will come.

If you are serious about wanting to be saved, please remember what I have said here. Act on it—honestly and with your whole heart—and you will be saved.

---

53   Luke 5:32

TO THOSE WHO PRAY -
SOME BROTHERLY ADVICE

L et me spend the rest of this short book speaking to those who do pray. I am sure that some people who read this are fully aware what prayer is, and that they have been adopted into God's family by his Holy Spirit. I want to offer people in this situation some words of brotherly advice and encouragement.

In the days of the tabernacle, there were very clear and careful instructions for the burning of incense. Not every kind of incense was acceptable. Let us take this as a reminder to be careful about how we pray. If I know anything of a Christian's heart, there are many believers who are often sick of their own prayers. We read the apostle Paul's words, 'when I want to do right, evil lies close at hand'—and those words feel particularly relevant and meaningful when we are on our knees.[54] We agree with David when he says, 'I hate the double-minded.'[55] We can sympathise with the poor

54   Romans 7:21
55   Psalms 119:113

Christian man who prayed, 'Lord, deliver me from all my enemies, and, above all, from that bad man myself!' It is common to be disheartened about our prayers.

Most Christians know that times of prayer can often feel like times of battle and conflict. This is not surprising—the Devil has a special anger towards us when he sees us on our knees. I think we should be very suspicious of prayers which cost us nothing and cause us no trouble at all. And I think we are very poor judges of how 'good' our prayers are. I suspect that prayers which please us least, may often please God most.

Allow me then, as a fellow traveller in the Christian life, to suggest some words of encouragement. One thing will all agree on for sure is this: we must pray! We cannot give up. We must go on.

I. PRAY WITH REVERENCE AND HUMILITY

So, first, let me encourage you to pray with both reverence and humility. Let us remember what we are before God. Speaking to him is solemn business. Beware of rushing carelessly and disrespectfully into his presence. Let us remind ourselves, 'I am on holy ground. This is the very gate of heaven. If I do not mean what I say, I am trifling with God. If I cherish sin in my heart, the Lord will not hear me.'

Notice how some Old Testament believers spoke to God:

> *Solomon reminds us, 'Be not rash with your mouth, nor let your heart be hasty to utter a word before God, for God is in heaven and you are on earth.'* [56]

> *When Abraham spoke to God, he said, 'I who am but dust and ashes.'* [57]

> *Similarly, when Job spoke, he said, 'I am of small account.'* [58]

Let us learn from their example.

2. BE 'SPIRITUAL' IN YOUR PRAYERS

I mean by this that we should always call on the Holy Spirit to help us in our prayers. We must beware of mere formality and saying our prayers without thinking. It is quite possible to get into the habit of praying with words that sound spiritual and seem very Biblical, yet, in reality, they are an empty shell. They are prayers prayed without thinking, without feeling, without engaging our hearts, like an aeroplane on autopilot.

I want to raise this point very carefully and sensitively. I realise that there are some things we need to ask the Lord for each day, so some repetition is inevitable. Using the same words each day—such as the Lord's Prayer, for example—does not necessarily mean that our prayers are not heartfelt and spiritual. The world, the Devil and our hearts are the same each day, and that means that

---

56   Ecclesiastes 5:2
57   Genesis 18:27
58   Job 40:4

we will need to pray over the same old ground in our prayers. But I do say this: we must take great care. If we use exactly the same outline day by day, let us make sure that it is clothed and filled by the Holy Spirit as much as possible.

Some people like to make use of written prayers from a book. Personally, I do not think that it is a particularly helpful habit. If we can tell our doctors about our aches and pains without a book, we ought to be able to speak with God about the state of our souls without one. If someone has broken their leg, I do not object to them using crutches when they are first recovering. It is much better to use crutches than not walking at all. But if I saw someone on crutches year after year, I would not congratulate them! I would like to see them strong enough to throw their crutches away.

3. GIVE PRAYER A REGULAR SLOT IN YOUR DAY

Next, I suggest to you that it is most important to make prayer a regular part of your day. I would also like to point out the value of having regular, set times in the day for prayer. It can help us a lot. God is a God of order. Disorder must be one of the fruits of sin. But I do not want to make rules just for the sake of it. I will just say this: it is essential to your soul's health to make prayer part of every twenty-four hours in your life. Just as you make time for eating, sleeping and work, so also make time for prayer. Choose your own times. At the very least, we should speak with God in the morning before we speak with the world; and speak with God at night, after we have done with the world.

But resolve in your own mind, that prayer is to be one of the important things of every day. Do not push prayer into a corner. Do not sweep it under the carpet. Do not give it the scraps and leftovers of your day. Whatever else you make a priority of, make a priority of prayer.

4. DO NOT GIVE UP

Next, I encourage you to persevere in prayer. Do not give up! Having taken up the habit, do not stop! Your heart will sometimes say to you, 'You have had family prayers; it will not hurt much if you do not bother with your own private prayers' or 'You prayed at the prayer meeting, you do not need to pray by yourself.' Your body will sometimes say, 'You are unwell, or tired—you do not need to pray.' Your mind will sometimes say, 'You have got important work to do, just pray very quickly.' Consider suggestions like these as coming directly from the Devil. They are all basically saying to us: 'Do not bother take care of your soul; it is fine to neglect it.' I am not saying that prayers should always be exactly the same length, but I do say, do not let any excuse encourage you to give it up.

Paul said, 'continue steadfastly in prayer' and 'pray without ceasing.'[59] He did not mean that Christians should be on their

---

59   Colossians 4:2, 1 Thessalonians 5:17

knees all the time, as an ancient sect called the Euchitae apparently thought! But he did mean that our prayers should be like the Old Testament practice of continuous burnt offerings, something that was steadily persevered at, day after day. Our prayers should be like the fire on the altar, never completely going out. It should be like the seasons of the year—coming one after the other, in a continuous process, never stopping.

Do not forget that we can link together our morning and evening prayers with an endless chain of short 'arrow' prayers throughout the day. Even when we are with others, at work, walking along the street or at home, we can be praying silently, sending up little winged messengers to God. That is what Nehemiah did when he came into the presence of King Artaxerxes.[60]

Never think that time given to God is time that is wasted. A Christian who perseveres in prayer will find that they never lose out in the long run.

5. BE EARNEST IN PRAYER

My next encouragement to you is to make sure your prayers are heartfelt and earnest. We do not need to shout out or be loud and showy to prove that we are in earnest. But it is a good thing for our prayers to be passionate, fervent and warm. And it is good to ask ourselves if we are really interested in what we are saying and doing.

---

60   Nehemiah 2:4

Elijah 'prayed fervently.'[61] His prayers were not cold, sleepy, lazy or listless. When the Bible speaks about prayer, it speaks in terms of crying, knocking, wrestling, labouring and striving. They are all words of passion, fervency, persistence and hard work. And the Bible gives us plenty of examples of people who pray this way.

> *Jacob is one. He said to the angel at Penuel, 'I will not let you go, unless you bless me.'[62]*

Daniel is another. Listen to how he pleaded with God: 'O Lord, hear; O Lord, forgive. O Lord, pay attention and act. Delay not, for your own sake, O my God.'[63]

> *And, of course, our Lord Jesus Christ is another. In Hebrews, it says, 'In the days of his flesh, Jesus offered up prayers and supplications, with loud cries and tears.'[64]*

Sadly, so many of our prayers could not be described like this. They are so tame and lukewarm in comparison. God could be justified in asking us if whether we genuinely want what we are praying for.

We must try to put this right. In John Bunyan's book, *Pilgrim's Progress*, there is a character called Mercy who knocked as if she would die if she was not heard. Let us knock loudly at the door of grace as she did. Let us be sure in our own minds that cold prayers are like a sacrifice without fire.

61　　James 5:17
62　　Genesis 32:26
63　　Daniel 9:19
64　　Hebrews 5:7

The story is told of Demosthenes who was a great orator. A man came to him, asking if he would speak on his behalf, but Demosthenes did not really pay attention because the man explained his situation with such little earnestness. When the man realised that Demosthenes was not listening to him, he cried out with great anxiety that his situation was extremely important. 'Ah!' said Demosthenes, 'I believe you now.'

6. PRAY WITH FAITH

Next, I want to remind you about the importance of praying with faith. We must try to remember that our prayers are always heard. We must also remember that if we ask things according to God's will, our prayers will always be answered. Do not forget Jesus' command: 'I tell you, whatever you ask in prayer, believe that you have received it, and it will be yours.'[65]

A feather is essential to an arrow—without it, the arrow will not hit its target. So too faith is essential to prayer, ensuring that our prayers can hit the mark. We need to develop this habit of praying with faith. We can start by using the Bible's promises in our prayers. For example, 'Lord, here is your own word, a promise that you have made. Do for us as you have said you would.' This was what Jacob, Moses and David did. Psalm 119 is full of these kind of prayers; when David asks God for things, he asks 'according to your word.'

---

65   Mark 11:24

Above all, we should develop the habit of expecting answers to our prayers. We should be like a merchant who sends his ships to sea and expects a return, or someone who expects a profit from an investment. We should not be satisfied unless we see answers to our prayers. This in an area where we Christians fall so short. The church at Jerusalem prayed endlessly for Peter when he was in prison, but when their prayers were answered, they could hardly believe it![66] Robert Traill, a 17th century Scot, said, 'There is no surer mark of trifling in prayer, than when men are careless what they get by prayer.'

7. BE BOLD IN PRAYER

My next encouragement to you is to be bold in your prayers. I am not talking about being over-familiar, which is totally inappropriate. But there is a 'holy boldness' which is a good thing. I mean boldness like Moses showed when he pleads with God not to destroy Israel. 'Why should the Egyptians say, 'With evil intent did he bring them out…? Turn from your burning anger and relent from this disaster against your people.'[67]

Or what about when the Israelite people were defeated and Joshua asks with great boldness: 'And what will you do for your great name?'[68] The great Reformer Martin Luther was also known for his boldness. One person who heard him praying said this: 'What a spirit, what a confidence was in his very expressions!

---

66   Acts 12:15
67   Exodus 32:12
68   Joshua 7:9

With such a reverence he sued, as one begging of God, and yet with such hope and assurance, as if he spoke with a loving father or friend.'

Robert Bruce, a great Scottish Christian of the 17th century, was also said to have this boldness in prayer. His prayers were described as 'bolts shot up into heaven.'

I am afraid most of us fail badly at this. We completely forget what amazing privileges we have as Christian believers. We do not plead with the Lord as much as we could, and say, 'Lord, we are your own people, aren't we? It is for your glory that we should be made holy, so please make us holy. Surely it is for your honour that the gospel should spread and the church should grow.'

8. REMEMBER FULLNESS IN PRAYER

Now I want to remind you about the importance of 'fullness' in prayer. What exactly do I mean? Think of the mistake the Pharisees made—they prayed long prayers to impress other people. Jesus tells us not to pray lengthy, repetitive prayers. But, on the other hand, he also teaches us that praying for a long time is a good thing. Remember how he spent all night in prayer to his Father. I do not think we are in danger of praying too much! It is much more likely that today's Christians run the danger of praying too little. The actual amount of time that many Christians give to prayer is very little indeed.

I worry that most people's private prayer is painfully inadequate and limited—it is just about enough to prove they are still alive, not much more than that. They really do not seem to want very much from God. They seem to have little to confess, little to ask for and little to thank him for. I am sure you can see that this is altogether wrong!

You often hear Christians complaining that things are not going well for them. They say that they are not growing as much as they want to. I suspect the problem is that they are, in fact, growing just as much as they have asked... In other words, not a lot. Is it not true that many people have little because they ask for little? The reason for their weakness is to be found in their own hurried, meagre, stunted, miserable, pitiful, small-minded, feather-weight prayers. They do not have because they do not ask. We are not limited by Christ, we are limited by our own actions! The Lord is generous and wants to give us good things: 'Open your mouth wide, and I will fill it,' he says in the Psalms.[69] But we behave rather like one of the kings of Israel who was told by God's prophet to strike the ground with an arrow. Instead of persevering, he gave up after just three strikes.[70] The prophet Elisha was angry with him and told him that if he had continued and not stopped, he would have achieved great success in battle.

We do not need to worry about praying too *much*; it would be a good thing if we were concerned about praying too little.

---

69   Psalms 81:10
70   2 Kings 13

9. BE SPECIFIC IN PRAYER

My next piece of encouragement to you is about the importance of being specific in prayer.

We should not be satisfied with praying vague, general prayers. We should explain our specific requests to the Lord on his throne of grace. A vague confession that we are sinners should not satisfy us. We should tell God about the particular sins where our conscience tells us we are most guilty.[71] A general prayer for holiness should not satisfy us either. We should specify the qualities and graces we feel most need for.[72] An unfocused prayer telling the Lord we are in trouble should not be enough for us. We should describe our troubles to him and tell him all about the difficulties we are facing. That is what Jacob did when he was frightened—he tells God exactly what he fears his brother Esau might do.[73] That is what Eliezer did when he was looking for a wife for his master's son—he lays before God precisely what he wants.[74] This is what Paul did when he was suffering from a 'thorn in the flesh'—he begged the Lord to take it away.[75] This is true faith and confidence.

We should remember that nothing is too small or insignificant to talk to God about. What would you think of the patient who told the doctor they were ill, but never explained exactly what was wrong? What would you think of a wife who told her husband

---

71   See, for example, Colossians 3:5-10
72   See, for example, Galatians 5:22-23
73   Genesis 32:11
74   Genesis 24:12
75   2 Corinthians 12:8

she was unhappy, but would not say why? What would you think of a child who told his father he was in trouble, but gave no details? Please remember this wonderful truth: Christ is the perfect father to all his people, he is the most eminent doctor for our hearts, he is the true bridegroom of the soul. Let us show that we understand and appreciate this by being unreserved in the way we communicate with him. Let us have no secrets from him. Let us share our hearts with him.

10. REMEMBER THE IMPORTANCE OF INTERCESSION

Next, I want to remind you of the importance of intercession in our prayers. I am talking about praying for the needs of others, for our world, for our church. We are all naturally selfish and selfishness tends to stick to us, even when we are converted. We naturally think only of our own souls, our own spiritual difficulties, our own progress in the faith, and we forget others.

We need to watch out for this and work against it, not least in our prayers. We should aim to widen our horizons. We need to stir ourselves up to name others before the throne of grace, and not just ourselves. We should try to carry in our hearts those who do not know Christ, those who do trust Christ, our world, our country and its rulers, the congregation we belong to, the homes we are part of, our friends and relations, our colleagues and neighbours.

We should pray and plead for each one of these. This is real love. Do you realise that the way to show true love for someone is to pray for them? Praying for others is the best thing for our souls: it enlarges our hearts and deepens our concern for others. Praying for others is the best thing for the church: it is the fuel for spreading the gospel. Those who *pray* (as Moses did on the mountain) do as much as those who fight in the thick of the battle (as Joshua did). We have the opportunity to be like Christ in this. He lifts the names of his people before his Father. What a privilege to be a little like our Lord Jesus! And this is a vital way that you can truly help the minister of your church. I am a minister myself and, if it were up to me to choose a congregation, I would always choose a congregation that prays.

II. BE THANKFUL IN YOUR PRAYERS

I want to encourage you to be thankful in prayer. I am fully aware that asking God for things is one thing, and praising him is another. But I see such close a connection between prayer and praise in the Bible, that I would not call something true prayer if there was no thankfulness in it. Paul chooses his words carefully when he says:

> 'in everything by prayer and supplication with thanksgiving let your requests be made known to God.'[76]

---

76   Philippians 4:6

He reminds the Colossians: 'Continue steadfastly in prayer,
being watchful in it with thanksgiving.'[77]

It is because of God's mercy that we are not in hell. It is because of his mercy that we have the certain hope of heaven. It is because of his mercy that we live in a land with religious freedom. It is because of his mercy that we have been called by his Holy Spirit, and not left to suffer the consequences of our own actions. It is because of his mercy that we are alive and have opportunities to glorify God.

Surely these thoughts should flood our minds whenever we speak with God. Surely we should never open our lips in prayer without thanking God for his grace which he gives freely to us, and for his loving-kindness which goes on forever. I do not believe there has ever been a noteworthy Christian who was not full of thankfulness. The apostle Paul hardly ever writes a letter without beginning with thankfulness. Men like George Whitefield and Edward Bickersteth were always overflowing with thankfulness. If we are to be bright and shining lights in our world, we must develop a spirit of praise and thankfulness. And above all, let our prayers be thankful prayers.

12. WATCH OUT!

Lastly, I want to remind you to watch out when it comes to your praying. Prayer is one of those things where it is particularly important to be on our guard. True faith begins with prayer, and it

---

77   Colossians 4:2

is with prayer that it flourishes. But beware: this is where faith can begin to decay. If you were to tell me about a man or woman's prayers, I would soon tell you how things are with their soul. Prayer is like our spiritual pulse. Our prayers are a measure of our spiritual health, like a spiritual health check. A person's prayer life opens a window into our hearts and shows whether our soul is healthy or dangerously ill.

I beg you, let us keep a constant watch upon our private devotions. Here is the heart of the matter, the real backbone of our Christianity. Sermons, books, church meetings, singing praises to God and the company of other Christians are all good things in their way, but they will never make up the chasm that opens up if we neglect private prayer.

Make sure you work out the kinds of places, situations, friends and things that turn your heart and emotions away from God, that make your prayers a burden to you, that make you neglect your times of prayer. When you identify those things, be on your guard! In the same way, notice carefully which friends and activities leave your soul in its best condition, that make you most ready to speak with God. Stick closely to those people and those things!

If you will take care of your prayers, I am confident that nothing will go very wrong with your soul.

I offer you these thoughts for your careful consideration. I hope I have done so with humility. I know that I need to be reminded of these truths more than anyone else I know. I do believe them to be God's own truth, and I long for myself and my loved ones to feel the importance of these realities more and more. I long for the times we live in to be praying times. I long for today's Christians to be praying Christians. I long for today's church to be a praying church. My heart's desire and prayer in writing this short book is to encourage a spirit of prayerfulness. I long that those who have never prayed should start right now! I long that those who do pray should know that they are not praying in vain.

Your affectionate friend

J C Ryle

This short book was written many years ago – but its message is as relevant as ever. The author presents us with a simple but direct challenge: 'Do you pray?' He does so with gentleness, humility, clarity, encouragement and a striking lack of guilt-trips! Read it and be inspired to grow in your relationship with our Lord Jesus Christ.

This edition takes Ryle's very beautiful 19th century prose and revises it slightly to make it more accessible to 21st century readers. If you would like to read it in his original words, it is available free online at: www.tracts.ukgo.com/john_charles_ryle.htm